by Jim Fremont
illustrated by Bill Morrison

Scott Foresman

Editorial Offices: Glenview, Illinois • New York, New York
Sales Offices: Reading, Massachusetts • Duluth, Georgia
Glenview, Illinois • Carrollton, Texas • Menlo Park, California

RING!

School was out. It was winter vacation!

I raced home. I couldn't wait to find out what we'd do this week. Mom and Pop always had great plans. Would we strap on snowshoes and hike to the North Pole? Would we learn to walk a tightrope?

Unfortunately . . .

Mom and Pop had a work emergency.

"I'm sorry, Marco," Pop said. "A grizzly escaped from the park. We have to find it. We'll make it up to you this summer."

I shrugged. But I was disappointed. Then the phone rang. Dad answered it.

Fortunately . . .

it was one of my uncles.

He wanted me to spend my vacation with him.

I've got four uncles. One is an astronaut. One is a deep-sea diver. One is a lumberjack.

"Is it Uncle Hank? Is it Uncle Jake? Is it Uncle Pete?" I asked.

Unfortunately . . .

it was Uncle Bob, the bookkeeper.

Don't get me wrong. I love Uncle Bob. But he works all day in an office, adding and subtracting numbers. I like math. But this was my vacation!

Fortunately . . .

Uncle Bob was going to visit Uncle Pete.

Uncle Pete is the lumberjack. He needed to get the money to build a new bunkhouse.

Uncle Bob and I took off.

The skies were clear all the way to the horizon. I looked down. As we flew farther north, there were fewer houses. Then there were no houses, just trees. Miles and miles of trees!

Unfortunately . . .

the plane started to buck and shake.

"What's wrong?" I shouted over the noise.

Uncle Bob checked dials and turned knobs.

"I don't know. It's not good, though."

He asked me to look behind my seat.

"There should be a box with parachutes in it,"
he said.

Fortunately . . .

I found the box stuck under my seat.

   Unfortunately, there was only one parachute
in the box.

   Fortunately . . .

Uncle Bob and I are quite light.

The plane's engine began to cough. Then it stopped. We put on the parachute and jumped.

Unfortunately . . .

we landed in a great forest full of giant timber.

How would anyone ever find us? How would we ever be able to hike to safety? We didn't even have snowshoes.

Fortunately . . .

when we turned around, we saw we were near
Uncle Pete's logging camp.

In fact, we could even see Uncle Pete, waving
from the top of a big boulder.

"HELLO!" he hollered.

Unfortunately . . .

he was holding a very big ax.

    It hit the tree he was chopping down.

    The tree wobbled.

    It teetered.

    It tipped.

    It crashed down toward the ground.

    Fortunately . . .

it missed Uncle Pete.

It missed everyone else as well.

It missed the camp.

It missed the tool shed.

Unfortunately . . .

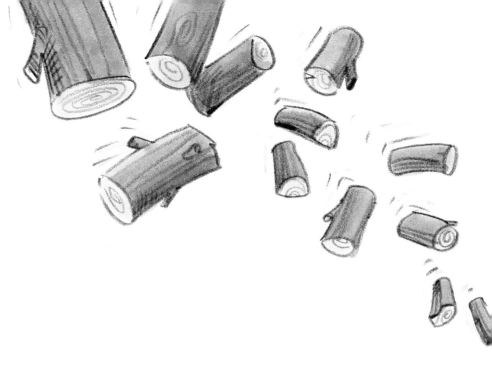

it hit a giant pile of wood.

About twenty cords of it!

All the logs in that pile flew up, up, up in the air. They spun, tumbled, and bounced. They made a sound like thunder. At last they fell back down.

Fortunately . . .

the logs landed neatly in a perfect square.

It was the size of a bunkhouse. It was the shape of a bunkhouse. It even had a cord of stove wood neatly stacked outside.

Uncle Pete's money troubles were over. He had a new bunkhouse for free!

Unfortunately, that bunkhouse had a growling grizzly trapped inside.

Fortunately . . .

my mom and pop were on the job!

Soon that grizzly was locked up tight.

And vacation wasn't over yet. Uncle Bob and I decided to visit Uncle Jake and Uncle Hank. Maybe they needed help too.

You know what? I think I'd like to be a bookkeeper when I grow up. Fortunately, I have a great teacher!